Books written by MARC KAMINSKY

Poetry
Daily Bread
A Table with People
A New House
Birthday Poems

Prose
What's Inside You It Shines Out of You

Theatre Pieces by Marc Kaminsky
Casualties
Worksong (*in collaboration with the
Talking Band*)
Terminal (*in collaboration with Susan
Yankowitz and the Open Theatre*)

Books Edited by Marc Kaminsky
The Uses of Reminiscence: New Ways of
Working with Older Adults
The Book of Autobiographies
The Journal Project: Pages from the
Lives of Old People

THE
ROAD
FROM
HIROSHIMA

Marc Kaminsky

SIMON AND SCHUSTER · NEW YORK

COPYRIGHT © 1984 BY MARC KAMINSKY
ALL RIGHTS RESERVED
INCLUDING THE RIGHT OF REPRODUCTION
IN WHOLE OR IN PART IN ANY FORM
PUBLISHED BY SIMON AND SCHUSTER
A DIVISION OF SIMON & SCHUSTER, INC.
SIMON & SCHUSTER BUILDING
ROCKEFELLER CENTER
1230 AVENUE OF THE AMERICAS
NEW YORK, NEW YORK 10020
SIMON AND SCHUSTER AND COLOPHON ARE REGISTERED
TRADEMARKS OF SIMON & SCHUSTER, INC.
DESIGNED BY EVE METZ
MANUFACTURED IN THE UNITED STATES OF AMERICA

1   3   5   7   9   10   8   6   4   2

LIBRARY OF CONGRESS CATALOGING IN PUBLICATION DATA
KAMINSKY, MARC, 1943–
    THE ROAD FROM HIROSHIMA.

POEMS.
    BIBLIOGRAPHY: P.
    1. HIROSHIMA-SHI (JAPAN)—BOMBARDMENT, 1945—
POETRY.   2. ATOMIC BOMB VICTIMS—POETRY.   I. TITLE.
PS3561.A418R6   1984   811'.54   84–5591
ISBN: 0-671-53055-0

ACKNOWLEDGMENTS

Parts of this work first appeared in magazines. I would like to thank the editors of: *Socialist Review* ("Questions," "Encounter," "The Burden," "Congregation," "Dragonflies") and *New Letters* (Section 13 of "White Blouse" was first published under the title "Barrier"; Section 2 of "Memory" was first published under the title "Mourning").

Twelve of the thirty-four poems comprised the text of "The Road from Hiroshima," a half-hour radio program produced by Dennis Bernstein with Connie Blitt for "New Letters on the Air" and broadcast over National Public Radio to 200 stations throughout the U.S.A. on Hiroshima Day, August 6, 1983: "New Year's Day, 1945," "The Bombing of Hiroshima," "August 6, 1945," "A White Blouse," "Corpse Duty," "The Doctor," "Days of Terror," "Every Day," "To Give Comfort," "The German Missionary," "Lauds," and "The Witness." The text was set to music by Steve Browman and read by Diane Dowling and Arthur Strimling. The production was directed by Arthur Strimling.

With solidarity and gratitude I acknowledge my debt to Masuji Ibuse's *Black Rain*; Tatsuichiro Akizuki's *Nagasaki 1945*; Michihiko Hachiya's *Hiroshima Diary*; *Unforgettable Fire: Pictures by Atomic Bomb Survivors*; Robert Jay Lifton's *Death in Life: Survivors of Hiroshima*; and John Hersey's *Hiroshima*. The Notes identify quotations contained within the text and cite the sources on which individual poems are based.

I have to thank two poets whose very different readings of the manuscript were especially helpful. Mark Weiss gave the poems the kind of close reading and practical criticism from which any work can only prosper. Alan Feldman's wise and incisive questioning of the overall structure pushed me toward a fuller realization of the work. Madelaine Santner, Allan Appel, and Amy Vladeck Heinrich contributed valuable notes and comments, which helped me in revising the text. I have also to thank Polly Howells and Eric Werthman whose generous support provided much-needed writing time. The Brookdale Center on Aging of Hunter College granted me a flexible work schedule, without which sustained research and writing would not have been possible. Dennis Bernstein and Connie Blitt appeared at just the right moment to take some of this writing from my hands and transmit it into the hands of others. Their collaboration with actors and musicians gave me a sense that I had done what I set out to do: to write a kind of poetry that I had learned about from Brecht: work that is of use in addressing great social questions. Finally, Steve Browman and Arthur Strimling did what no writer can do for himself: completed the book by receiving it into their lives. Through them, the work began to lead what Eugenio Montale calls "the second life of art: its obscure pilgrimage through the conscience and memory of men [and women], its entire flowing back into the very life from which art itself took its first nourishment."

—M.K.

FOR STEVE BROWMAN AND ARTHUR STRIMLING

CONTENTS

QUESTIONS   15

I. FIELD OF LOST EDGES

    New Year's Day, 1945   19
    May 7, 1945   23
    July 1, 1945   34

II. THE PASSION

    The Bombing of Hiroshima   41
    August 6, 1945   41
    A White Blouse   44
    Encounter   55
    The Burden   57
    Congregation   61
    Dragonflies   63

III. DISTANCES

    Corpse Duty   67
    The Walker   68
    The Bones   68
    The Homeowners   70

Them   71

The Doctor   73

Days of Terror   73

The Refugee   77

IV. In Mourning

To Give Comfort   81

Memory   86

Carrying My Brother   88

Every Day   89

Every Month   91

Every Year   91

The Voice Underneath the Burning House   92

The German Missionary   93

V. Watchman: from the Journals of Nakajima Hiroshi

Nightwatch   97

Lauds   101

Surrender   102

First Taste of Prosperity   104

Responsibilities   105

Walking Ghosts   106

The Witness   107

NOTES   109

SOURCES   119

We are all survivors of Hiroshima.

—Robert Jay Lifton

It may be only by descending into this hell in imagination now that we can hope to escape descending into it in reality at some later time. The knowledge we thus gain cannot in itself protect us from nuclear annihilation, but without it we cannot begin to take the measures that can actually protect us.

—Jonathan Schell

QUESTIONS

Nakajima Hiroshi

If I shriek
who will hear me
if I don't
break the silence in which diatribes
pile up, who will
hear me
if I speak normal
words in the normal
order

who will hear me

if I make poems
of what I saw and heard on the road
from Hiroshima

will I disturb
the dead

will I
be a merchant of our disaster

if I fail
to work all the horror
into a play
of voices in which the living and the dead
live again

who will forgive me

I·Field of Lost Edges

NEW YEAR'S DAY, 1945

1.

The screeching alarm bells
and rattle
of antiaircraft fire

woke me at three this morning.
The enemy planes
had already passed over

our house and were dropping
incendiary bombs
in the distance.

After the all-clear
my daughters went up to Gobenden shrine
to pray.

Last night the temple bells
that signal the end of the year
did not sound.

2.

And it began to snow
just before dawn.
Bit by bit, in unison, the sky

and the earth became one
color, and the seven rivers
froze

in the afternoon
the snowfall grew heavier.
From the hills at Futaba-no-Sato

I looked down at Hiroshima
and I saw the many
bridges of the city

bleed
into the white
rivers

and the rivers meld
with the unaccustomed whiteness
of the streets

and the sun breaks
through
onto this field of lost edges

turning it
into a blinding
sheet of light.

3.

"What can this mean, snowfall
in January?"
They walked side by side

with their heads bowed, speaking
in whispers:
old and young, walking

home from the factories, across
Aioi Bridge.
"When was the last time

this happened? Snow
on the Inland Sea? In
the warmth of our winter?"

The old ones tried to remember
details of the storm
that befell their grandparents—

and what followed that
canceling of our climate?
The young ones insisted

"It is not a sign
that some catastrophe will come
before the year is out."

In whispers, the questions.
In whispers, the answers
the repetitions. . . .

"It is an omen
that the B-29s will continue
to pass

over Hiroshima without dropping
their load.
Our luck will hold good."

4.

Listening
as always to the conversations
among which I walk

I measure the intervals
between these exchanges of
the correct views.

Each day they get longer.
The list
of things we dare not say

has gotten so huge
it blots out nearly all discussion.
Once we had victories

of the Imperial Army
to talk about.
Then there was rationing

then factory work
then the black market
then the air raids

but all that was used up.
Today we have snow in January.
Walking side by side

with their heads bowed
the young and the old have trouble
managing even a few words

of encouragement: they sputter
and fall silent.
And that's when I hear

them crying
that the war has gone on too long
that our luck can't hold

that holidays can't be told
apart from days of hunger
and every day beaten

into nightmare by the erratic
air-raid warnings and lack
of sleep

the endless drills and hours
of "volunteer labor"—nothing exists now
but the war.

In the snow I heard them crying
out against
the monotony, the terror. . . .

MAY 7, 1945

1.

This morning—six small clams.
I dug them
out of the sand under Miyuki Bridge.

My daughters
foraged for wild plants
near the banks of the Ota

they found only some grubs
and pigweed—
even their secret place

was picked clean.
So my wife set out
with our youngest one's

best summer kimono—
the last fine piece of
anything we had to trade—

and made the rounds
of all the neighboring farms
she sold it

for a cake of bean curd
two Chinese cabbages
six carrots, a bunch of spinach

and four eggplants—
all this
because my sister arrived today

and we didn't want her
coming under our roof
without a proper welcome.

2.

Three steps
out of the train
as she embraced me

Misao whispered,
"Do you still eat here
in Hiroshima?"

We walked
for miles beyond the city
and in a scorched field

where only the crows
could overhear us
I answered, "No."

3.

And she told me
that her husband
had not been captured

he was dead
and her house
destroyed

after the latest raid
Tokyo
was a plain of broken objects

with patches
of red lying here and there
—rusting

refrigerators and safes
everything flammable
gone

the rest looted
she had nothing
not even a photograph

to place on a family altar
nothing
remained of her life

in Tokyo
her daughter had been seized
by the Kempei-tai

for making "defeatist remarks"
marched into a meadow
made to sit down

and pummeled
from early morning
until late at night.

"Don't think I believe,"
she added quickly, "that Japan
is going to lose the war."

She looked at me piercingly.
"Misao!" I cried. "I'm your brother!"
And she dropped her eyes.

4.

Walking
through the streets
where we were children

together
thirty years ago
she stopped abruptly

at the edge of tears
Oh Misao
what

thoughts were trembling
into your face
just then

a blast
of martial music
froze

everything she was
about to say
she threw

her hands up to her ears
then dropped them
abruptly

as a familiar voice
began speaking
through shuttered windows

and suddenly it was everywhere
at once—
rapid, staccato, bellowing

from radios
that are always on
from every house and shop

on every street
all other voices silent
to hear the war news.

5.

Every hour
we hear a fantastic number
of B-29s

has just been shot down.
And every night
another Japanese city goes under.

The Air Force says
its fighters possess godlike powers.
The Navy says

its ships are invincible.
On the ruined streets
of our cities

the placards say:
Give cotton! The Army
needs it for gunpowder!

Yesterday
every newspaper ran
the same banner headline:

THE TIME TO GRASP VICTORY IS NOW!
How is this possible
when the rations

that keep us alive
make us sick
with constant diarrhea?

6.

Passing the East Parade Ground
we saw new recruits
whom the newspapers call "a wave

of human bullets
that will drive the invader
into the sea"—

they are a line of older men
being trained
to charge the American Army

with bamboo spears.
The officer, screaming
slogans at them

slapped them on the legs
and buttocks
with the side of his sword.

Emaciated
a few of them maimed
too weak

to knock over the targets
at which they repeatedly
threw their spears

they hurled their bodies
against the line of straw men
who nonetheless did not fall.

7.

And so we came back to my place
in Senda-machi
a crowd of neighbors was there

hungry for any news that the refugee
from Tokyo might be carrying.
They blocked the door, crying, "Tell us

is it true that the Emperor's palace
hasn't been hit?"
But Kyoji appeared out of nowhere—

at the moment I thought nothing
of his having spirited himself out
of a steel mill 100 miles away.

Giving his deepest bow
and speaking in Tokyo dialect
perhaps out of deference

to Misao, he said, "Good
neighbors, our sister
will speak with each of you

tomorrow when she is rested."
And ceremoniously
he ushered her into the house.

8.

We sat down formally
on our heels.
Yoshiko, Nanae, and Misa

served the meal
that my wife had conjured up:
a tempura

made of eggplant and cabbage,
a bit of bean curd, broiled
with salt, two

raw slices of carrot—
a great luxury—
and a bowl of barley.

The clams, six
little mandalas, six
reminders

of days of peace
were beautifully displayed
—three apiece—

on the plates
of my sister and brother.
And so we entered the circle

of the comfort of food.
But Yoshiko could not
contain herself: she asked ,

"Where is your daughter?
In good health?"
"In Tokyo," Misao answered.

Suddenly Kyoji shifted
to the informal
cross-legged position

he said,
"For one night let us forget
the war

I have something
which can draw
out forgotten feelings

and give a foretaste of
how we will live
when it ends."

And he pulled
a bottle
out from under his jacket:

"Gentian bitters!
Homemade. Distilled
from a liter

of medicinal alcohol
that I managed to lay my hands on.
Bring water, Yoshiko!

And glasses.
There will be a faint
bitterness at first

but if you wash it down
with water
it will pass in a moment."

The movements of his hands
were deferential
as he stirred the mixture—

seven parts water
to three parts of the
brew

he was serving us.
Bowing to me, he said,
"To your health, Hiroshi."

"To our health," I answered
touching my glass against his
"and to the health of everyone here."

"Two glasses of this,"
Kyoji said, "will get you
quite happy

and if you think you are happy
then you are—in a way—
happy."

One by one
we drank to each other's health
soon everyone was

in a more relaxed position:
sister and brother and brother
and sister-in-law and wife

and daughters and aunt and nieces
and uncle and parents—
all gathered at one table.

That night
while we were together
again

it seemed as though a line
had been drawn
around my house

and for as long as we sat there
banqueting
the war couldn't come in.

JULY 1, 1945

1.

Used up the last of our salt
with tonight's meal
at sundown we crawled

into our bedrolls, hoping
to get some rest
before the air-raid sirens . . .

our fatigue
is so vast
it has gotten the better of

our fears. We yearn
for one thing only: a night
of sleep.

Waving her arms
above the paraphernalia
we keep around each bedroll—

her bamboo life raft, emergency
bag of clothing, first-aid kit
her little box of food—

Yoshiko cried, "Let them
get it over with!
We've been at it so long—

let it come! tonight! .
let the worst of it
be finished!"

And I understood. More
than that:
I too was ready

to imagine
that with four sticks
of bamboo

and a few pieces
of cotton
we would be invulnerable.

2.

At ten-thirty
the air-raid warning sounded
ten minutes later

it became a full-scale
alarm
at least 100 B-29s

flew directly over us
and then it began—
red skies on the horizon

the destruction
of the sheltered and prosperous
port of Kure.

3.

Awake the whole night
watching the mass of flames
grow mountainous

I thought: centuries of work—
a city made of paper and wood—
will be gone by daybreak.

At my desk, my hands
tremble. I can do nothing
but helplessly record

these events
in a journal I have to keep
hidden.

If I live
to have grandchildren
ask me about the war

I will tell them:
it wasn't possible to write
let alone publish

the truth. To speak
sometimes meant
never to speak again.

For years I did nothing
but smoke
and read the newspaper

and walk around in the city.
And I kept track of everything
I saw and heard.

II·The Passion

THE BOMBING OF HIROSHIMA

The Shopkeeper's Assistant

It happened something like an electric short
a bluish-white light
blanked out everything
there was noise more than the ground beneath me
could take I felt great heat
even inside the house
I was underneath the destroyed house
I thought: a bomb
has fallen directly upon me our house
has been directly hit I became furious
roof tiles and walls everything black covering me
I screamed from all around I heard screaming
then I felt a kind of danger
unable to do anything by my own power
I didn't know where I was or what I was under
I thought: I'm going to die.

AUGUST 6, 1945

The German Missionary

A terrible flash
rushed from east to west
and became everywhere
at once

there was a wave
of heat
that reached under my clothes
and scorched my skin

it passed
the sky held its breath
trees broke
into flame

there was a blank
in time
then a huge boom
came thundering

toward the mountain
a violent rush of air
took my body
and flung it against the ground

my hair tangled in branches
a wall of wind
pressed my being
into the earth

there was a silence
then a series
of shattering sounds
a mass of clouds

rose
and climbed rapidly into the sky
a column of boiling
clouds

spread and climbed, erupted
unfolded sideways, constantly
changing shape and color
climbed higher and wider

then burst
at the summit
and put out a monstrous head
that loomed over everything

I looked out
over a ledge of rock
and what I felt then
and what I feel now

I can't explain
it was not shock
or horror
I became mute with

I could see streets
in the distance
a few buildings
standing

here and there
but Hiroshima didn't exist
I saw
Hiroshima did not exist.

A WHITE BLOUSE

1.

Not aware
of what I was doing
I jumped
down to the track and braced
myself against it

somebody fell on top of me, screaming
a stream of pebbles lashed my face
trying to scream
my tongue fought an eerie
weight and I couldn't
hear me

though I lay there shrieking with all
my strength

I found
I had stuffed a handkerchief into my mouth
and covered my eyes and ears
with my hands

2.

Even now
I can't remember
how I threw off the bodies that boxed me in
and got to my feet

how I thrust aside
the passengers swarming
against me

how I climbed back onto the platform

I took one step, then another

but they came upon me
like lava they scalded they knocked me
off-balance they carried me
toward the burning
cars

I hit against something hard

I threw my arms
around it
wrapped my legs around it
not aware
of what I was doing

I held on
as wave after wave beat against me
smashing my chin
against steel
pulling my arms from their sockets

my whole body racked
and numb
I clung
to that pillar

3.

Eventually it was quiet
I tried to open
my eyes
I thought: Lord
why have you blinded me?
I thought: this is happening
in a dream

then I saw a light brown haze
obscure everything
a chalky ash
fell through the air
there wasn't a soul on the platform

4.

but their shoes! hundreds
of shoes, left
and right separated
one from the other, confused
with clogs, strewn
among sandals and slippers

and all overturned
or turning this way
and that, half-buried
under a chaos of
hoods and parasols—

only the shoes and hats, shorn
of their people!

like headstones and footstones
marking

          the mass of
disappearance

5.

and I
the only one left?

6.

Black smoke rising
here and there
and Nakahiro-cho where my parents lived
already in flames—

apologizing in my heart
I turned away from their home
to seek shelter.

7.

Walls
on either side of the road torn down
stone walls and fences
                around each of the houses
demolished

brick walls, plasterboard, paneling, beams, blackened
window frames, rain doors, silk and gold
hand-painted screens

demolished!

leaving Yokogawa Station
I couldn't make out the road.

47

8.

I walked through what had once been
a house

and shreds of someone's daily routine—
a clock, an ironing board, a photograph
of a sailor carrying a boy on his back—
were visible
under broken roof-tiles

pieces of white blouse and mattress
shocked me, hanging
from telegraph poles

I cried, "Anyone here?"

just as
I realized I
was together with the dead
woman in her bedroom

only we weren't really inside the house

all the walls between outside
and inside missing

fire beginning to fan out before me
around me

everywhere was out-of-doors
and cemetery

9.

bits of sky
fluttered into view, were swallowed
and spat out elsewhere

light dropped through holes in the whirling
cloudcover

and I was not alone

climbing through the remains of a bathroom

a boy
clinging to an emergency
bucket of sand

I went
toward him, I wanted
to take his hand

but he shivered away from me
hugging his bucket

he must have grabbed it
when earth went up
in millions of pounds of light

he walked unconsciously
pressing
this weight against him

as if it could keep him
from floating off—

another strand of black smoke

10.

And then
the debris was populated
naked
and half-naked men
and women
reeled against me

and a small voice under the wreckage—

only a pair of legs
could be seen

but a group
formed around the block of concrete
that sealed her in

pushing
in five different directions
we couldn't move it

"Forgive us," the others said

but I stayed
how long I can't say, praying
with her

"Help me
remove this stone," I pleaded

as naked
and half-naked men
and women
collided and sank
amid the debris

then I too went away

11.

One thing consoled me: my watch
was still ticking
it was 8:31! Only sixteen minutes
since the blast

I began counting footsteps
timing my progress

12.   8:50 A.M. near Yokogawa Station

Again
it comes back to me: the sensation
that this was only
my dream—

the thatched roof on fire

the peasant and his wife
moved deftly to salvage their household
furnishings, item
by item

but carrying
a great lacquered chest of drawers
they got stuck

no matter how they turned
and angled it
they couldn't come through

so they stood facing each other
with most of their movable
goods in their arms

the man taking a half-step to the left, slowly
the woman to the right
then back again
as if in a trance

a slow, solemn, mesmerizing dance
in the open doorway
as the cottage burned

nobody stopped to help them.

13.   Crossing Misasa Bridge, 9:15 A.M.

From a distance
I could see only the woman, lying
on her side
half-blocking
the other end of the bridge

and the refugees, as they approached
her, hesitated

one turned back
and ran toward the burning city

"What is it?" I cried

but she didn't answer

"You'll get past this," I told myself
"if you don't look!"

but after counting a hundred steps
afraid
something bad was about to happen
I dropped my hands

and a baby girl
was undoing the buttons
of her mother's blouse

I drew close
and I saw
her clutch at the breasts of a corpse
she looked up at me
terrified

What could I possibly do for her?

"Go on," I said to my legs
"step over the body
and go on."

14.   On the other side, 9:20 A.M.

A girl my age
was standing with vacant eyes in the middle
of the road
the great wound in her forehead
like a pomegranate
cracked open

instinctively
I ran
my fingers across the skin
of my face

when I looked
down at my hands
there was blood on them

so I got the mirror
out of my emergency kit
and located
a small cut on my eyebrow

which I washed with spittle

then I
did up my hair
in a handkerchief
neatly
and went on.

15.   9:40 A.M. at the bank of the Nagatsuka

I was wearing a white blouse
with a blue pattern
miraculously it was free
of dirt
and it didn't get torn

everyone else
was in rags and hurt
a woman
with the flesh of her side scooped out
and her ribs exposed
seeing me thread my way through the crowd
in my nice clothes
asked, "Can you help me?"

but a man came between us
and admonished her, saying, "Everyone
has the same pain as you.
Endure it
and we will find shelter."

16. 4:30 P.M.

I reached my aunt's village

and I went to the river
to wash my clothes

the moment
I dipped my blouse in the water
it fell apart.

ENCOUNTER

The Soldier

1.

A bald head
on the body of a boy screaming, "Ichiro!"

its features so swollen
they had all run
into an anonymous mass

and gigantic!

I stared
at its awful roundness and size
and its brown covering

as the body ran toward me

the burnt head
mounted on top screaming my name.

2.

Whatever you hear
about Hiroshima
whatever wild stories you hear

all of it happened.

3.

I grabbed a stick
planted my feet under my shoulders
and crouched

why
had I been singled out by this weird
assailant?

then it crashed into me
coiled its arms around me
tried to bury its head
in my stomach

I raised my stick and began
to pummel
its legs and buttocks
crying, "Let me go!"

In horror he cried, "Ichiro!
It's me! Kyuzo! Your brother!"

THE BURDEN

1.

He was the only one
making his way toward the city

blue-green fireballs
drifted around him

dim figures
moved in the darkness

against the injured sky
the injured began to appear

2.

He saw

3.

one without eyebrows
then one bald
and vomiting as she walked
then one with black skin

and one with the skin of her back
hanging down
like a sheet of wet newspaper
and one mumbling prayers

and one holding a clock
straight-armed in front of his body
its low clean ticking
uncanny as a gong

and one with the bone
showing through
at the shoulder, cradling
the lifeless arm in the good one

then one leading a child
by the hand, and finding
it wasn't hers
shaking it loose

and one who couldn't be seen
under a burning house
calling, "Help if you please!"
and a ginkgo tree

burnt through, carbonized
in the shape of a tree
its great roots thrust out
into the air

and a naked one carrying a corpse
and pleading for water
and one whose disheveled hair
was caked with blood

then an old one half-dragging
a woman whose head
rolled heavily back and forth
then one with a fishing rod

then one who halted, who would not
go on in the black rain
and one with a wheelbarrow
full of papers

and one in white trousers
who crept along
on all fours, noiselessly sobbing
and one whose legs pumped

furiously up and down
who was wedged in
with a group of the dead and dying
who got nowhere

4.

And as he ran
toward the city, lacerated
with shame
that he alone was unhurt

he turned to the left and the right
and he said as he ran
past each of them, "Excuse me
that I have no burden like yours."

5.

No one wept
no one screamed in pain
none of the dying
died noisily
not even the children
cried
no one spoke

All day they poured
into the grove by the river
to hide under green
leaves

and all day the unwounded one
brought them water

He could not tell
the living from the dead

he brought water
to the lips of each body
that lay there
and if one drank
that meant his suffering
had not yet ended

Over and over he had to tell himself
"These are human beings"
as he gave the bottle
to those whose faces had been blotted out

and sometimes
after they tried to take in some water
they raised their bodies a little
and bowed to him, in thanks

CONGREGATION

The Pastor

1.

A boy
who lay propped up against the skeleton
of a camphor tree
pointed at me
and shouted, "Look!
there's someone who isn't
wounded!"

Beside him
a woman lay staring up at the sky
her hands and feet
twitching
I asked, "Can I
bring you some water?"

and she didn't answer

2.

Nearby a man writhing
on the ground

I asked, "Is there anything
I can do . . .
anything at all . . ."

The smell
nearly drove me away
I put my palms
on the earth to stop
the vertigo

while he labored, writing
on the black earth,
"Kill me!"

and I felt bothered
that I was still alive

3.

Off to one side
in a ditch
where a great number of bodies floated
I saw someone who was still alive
clutch
at the limbs of the dead
and try to climb out

I grabbed his wrists
but the skin of his hands came off
in my hands
I was left
with a few glovelike pieces
and the raw flesh
clawed at the mud and the blue
smoke over the ditch
as he slipped back into the ditch

I lay down
with the others, thinking:
this is the time to die

but I couldn't die.

DRAGONFLIES

Nakajima Hiroshi

And I asked myself:
will I ever again find anything
to celebrate?

Then I remembered:

on the outskirts of the ruined city
all the houses collapsed
but leaving the suburb of Gion
I was greeted by
dragonflies
flitting this way and that, so quickly, above
emerald fields
of rice

And I hated myself, realizing
that even on the day of horrors
I rejoiced!

III · Distances

CORPSE DUTY

The Social Worker

On one of those nights
I met a soldier who had just returned to the city
where I for days had been losing
count of the hours, collecting and cremating
corpses

on the site of one of the burnt-out shrines
near Matoba Bridge
                            suddenly we saw
blue phosphorescent flames, slender blue flames
around the bodies of the dead

To those who had just come from the outside
it looked like a devastated plain on which the spirits
of our kin were leaving Hiroshima—
blue phosphorescent flames
are what we had always looked upon as spirits
rising from the dead

Yet I in those days had gone
into a state in which I feared nothing
the soldier fell
to the ground, unable to speak
or go on
I said: the dead
are still burning. In another hour
you will get used to it.

THE WALKER

There was no place for me
to put down my feet
I began walking over the bodies of the dead
and the disappointment in their eyes

they stared right through me
as if I were the one
who would never again walk
in a man's body

Yet if I had not become pitiless
I would not have been able to walk
through the city
looking for my wife and son

THE BONES

1.

In the vegetable garden
by the river
where hundreds of students burned
I scooped up two handfuls
of bone and ash

let it run through my fingers
into the urn
carried it back to the family
altar
and called it my son

2.

Others were more particular.
They stood before the walls of the dead
like petitioners seeking justice
and talked to the bones, expecting
a miracle.

"My son," they demanded,
"if you are here among this pile of bones,
move your finger a little,
so that I can tell it is you, my son—
I will take you home for proper burial."

3.

To preserve the old
distinctions
seemed ridiculous

after all the boundaries we had known
were exposed in an instant
tortured out of shape

or melted into barbarous shapes
like girders of the schoolhouse
turned

into the skeleton of something
monstrous, never-known-
before, extinct.

THE HOMEOWNERS

Along the main road out
of Hiroshima
all the shutters were closed.
So the wounded walked on

or lay down in front of the houses
that no cry
would open.
But at a dry-goods store

on this side of Mitaki Station
they found
a woman who had managed to sneak inside
and die in one of their closets.

The owner, annoyed
at this disagreeable consequence,
dragged the body out by its feet
which were bare

and filthy.
And his wife was distraught
and he was scandalized
when they saw

the corpse dressed in their
daughter's best
summer kimono—a wonderful
piece of work

which they instantly tore
off the dead body,
only to find
that it had no underwear on.

And they could feel only
how unlucky they were
till the priest came
and explained what had probably happened.

She must have been burnt out
of her home—a girl
of no more than sixteen years—
who fled

all the way from the city,
looking for something
to hide her nakedness
even before she sought water.

THEM

The Bargirl

There was no light at all every time
an oildrum exploded
the ground shook huge pillars
of smoke went up they broke

into a run they ran
a few feet then went back
to their dead walk
their eyes closed

they swayed to and fro pushed
they staggered in any direction
they were carried by the long lines leaving
Hiroshima

covered with black rain
with chalky ash there wasn't one
who wasn't bleeding the hands
the face the feet the anus

from any place it is possible
to bleed they bled
their mouths their eyes I am
still with them I see them

like walking ghosts their arms
bent forward like this
they had a special way of walking—
very slowly—like this—

if only
there were one or two of them!
but wherever I walked
I met these people

many of them
died along the road—
I myself
was one of them.

THE DOCTOR

Even those who looked like they were going to be spared
were not spared

Weeks after the bombing
after what turned out to be a deceptive period
of remission
many of the survivors began to develop
petechiae

I know it is terrible to say
but those spots were beautiful —
red, green, yellow, and black
all over the body

DAYS OF TERROR

Nakajima Hiroshi

1.

One by one
those who escaped with light injuries
began to sicken.

Nosebleeds, bloody vomit, bleeding
from the vagina,
bloodspots under the skin—

with these signs
the bomb took up its second life
among us. Without privacy

we open every fold
of our bodies to anyone
who happens to be looking,

hundreds of times a day, looking
for the hidden spot that tells
how soon

each of us is going to turn the mulberry
color of worms
and die.

2.

Nights
are endless, every night this
new death

draws refugees
to the hospital, the front
entrance and courtyard

covered each morning anew
with bloody feces,
corridors and stairwells

crowded with dying,
each in his own black cloud of flies.
And the odor!

On the night I pulled a clump
of hair out of my skull
I lost control

and I too lay there
in a pool
of self-loathing.

3.

Beyond
the hospital fence
near the outdoor bathtub

they built a makeshift
crematorium.
A burnt door serves as a bier.

Orderlies
have been working
fourteen hours a day

and can't keep up
with the dying—
they cram themselves in

to supply rooms, linen
closets, even the toilets,
collapse, moan briefly

and have to be carried out—
so much dead
weight.

Placed
on a pile of broken desks
and crates

covered
with a slab of sheet zinc
and set on fire.

Pestilence
resolved in a spiral
of smoke—

it smells like decaying
squid, or bad
sardines.

Yesterday
three soldiers stood around
the bonfire

with long bamboo poles
they poked
at the corpses

as they slipped off
the flame-cracked bed
of wood.

"How many today?"
A loud voice out of nowhere.
"Who's that?" a soldier shouted back.

It was one of the orderlies
soaking
in the hot bath,

he splashed and sighed
and traded
a few jokes with the soldiers

while the setting sun
looked on
serene as usual

and we sat at the window
eating the evening meal, oblivious
of the stench in our nostrils.

4.

And now I am bored by the stories
survivors tell
when they first arrive.

I turn
my back to the wall, bored.
Even so

I take down everything
they say, incessantly feeding the pages
of my diary.

THE REFUGEE

1.

I waited, my air-raid
hood covering most of the burn
and my head bowed

at the edge of my village I waited
one of the faceless ones

        they closed their gates against us
and turned their eyes

on the road
from Hiroshima I became invisible

then the black-market woman came by
I got up and said: Taka Mitsuda
I would be deeply obliged if you would bring me
a mirror

then I went back
into the fields

2.

Can this be my face?

Taking one end of a curled-up piece
of skin
I tugged at it gently
It hurt
which assured me
that the face giving me this wary look
was mine

How can this be? I thought
peeling away each purple-black ridge
a bit at a time
like you play with a loose tooth
hating and enjoying the pain
I stripped off all the dead skin

3.

And then I turned to face them

IV·In Mourning

TO GIVE COMFORT

Nakajima Hiroshi

1.

He tells me
he is a scrivener, for forty years
he has worked the corridors
of the law courts, writing
bills and pleas

but with a little volume of *Duino
Elegies* or satori
poems
in the left-hand pocket where everyone hides
his wallet
he would steal
an eternity between clients

walking with Basho
and Rilke
along the seven branches of the river

and in the hills
at Futaba-no-Sato
he saw the dragonflies' wings flash
fire

transmitting the sun

he bows his head

he tells me
he is sorry for talking too much

and he tells me
this story:

2.

In Danbara Shin-machi
he came
upon four girls at the side of the road
and he wouldn't have stopped
but
they were sitting in a circle
they were sitting and facing each other
in a circle
and this
struck him as a remarkable thing

more than that—
an act of resistance
something
like meditation
like women
in a temple courtyard

so he was drawn to them
and their eyes
unlike eyes of other victims
                    were open
they were
looking into each other's eyes

and this
more than anything else he saw that day
kept death from ascendancy
everywhere

He asked one of them where her home was

she said, "This is my home.
I am Yoshiko, oldest daughter
of the poet
Nakajima Hiroshi. If you meet my father
or mother
tell them not to waste time
looking for me
or Nanae or Misa or Aunt Misao.
We are all going to die
right here."

The others nodded in agreement

then the tears came
and he was helpless before them

Yoshiko said, "If you would shield us
from the sun,
if you would find a way to shield us
from the wind,
it would make us quite happy."

So he built them a lean-to
of straw mats
and a few sheets of corrugated steel

and he went inside
and sat with them for a while

in his lunch box—three ripe tomatoes
which he sliced into halves
and he squeezed the juice onto the lips
and into the mouths
of my daughters

83

and though they could barely swallow
each one mumbled
"Oishii! delicious!"

3.

Past one o'clock
Dr. Murai stops at my bedside
before going to sleep

He tells me, "Your daughters
had the good fortune not to die
like a piece of debris

a blackened tile

a piece of sentient debris

no longer human

Today I walked
through fields of carbonized flesh and rubble
and I thought: those
who had someone to cry for them
those
     who died hearing the Heart Sutra
chanted for them
or with any sign that their death
          concerned the living
those who were sheltered in any form
from the boundarylessness of
the A-bomb—
those few
died a happy death in Hiroshima.

4.

Days
of torrential rain
relieve us
of the August sun

weeds
and wild flowers
bloom
riotously

at their first
taste of
sweet potato
since the bombing

patients
throughout the ward
murmur
"Oishii!"

and I
startle everyone—and myself—
    crying
violently and without shame

for my daughters

MEMORY

The Soldier

1.

whatever I saw
wiped out
everything around it

but whatever grabbed
my attention
was too much to be
looked at

so that each horror
deleted all others
and itself

like the wind
that shrouded itself and the earth in a veil
of dust

2.

but afterward
walking that road in my mind's eye

I saw our house gone
into splinters

our great porcelain wine jar
into shards

all the comforting parts of my life
turned into missiles

that could no longer blind me—
and I looked into the wind's barrage

3.

awakened now
at any hour of the day
and rushed back onto the road to Kabe

fleeing Hiroshima

these are the things I am always leaving
behind—

a burning pine tree

fallen power lines

a field of smashed watermelons

a dead horse

a piece of wood stuck
in a woman's eye

naked girls
covering their breasts, and crying
"Stupid America!"

my brother Kyuzo
whose body I carried to the river
who lay in great anguish the whole night
he couldn't die

the hands of a baby
black arms lifted to the sky
her fingers on fire
burning with ten blue flames

CARRYING MY BROTHER

The Shopkeeper's Assistant

I am still on the road to the doctor's house
carrying my brother
in my arms
thinking: he is going to survive

He was five months old
and all I could give him was gruel—
thin gruel
there were no spots on his body

A week after the bomb fell
he began to look better
I was pleased—
he was the only one I had left

and while we were on the road
to the doctor's house
he died
I found two big spots on his bottom

And I have never been able to escape
my loneliness and fear
even now
I find myself going to the mirror

three and four times a day, dropping
my pants, and looking for purple spots
and always nervously touching
my hair, and checking my gums

never sure
where some sign of the disease
will show itself
I am always on the road to the doctor

EVERY DAY

The Old Woman

1.   Morning

I still keep two pillows
on your side of the bed
but instead of puffing them up every morning
my hands sink into them

and put back the impression
your head left
when you slipped noiselessly into the day
I was still asleep

when the bomb fell
and all that remained
of your body
was this hollow place.

2.   Afternoon

Anyone who might have seen you die
also evaporated.
I have no thought
of anything now but you.

You must have gone
from driving full speed across Aioi Bridge
to death
in an instant.

3. Night

They say your spirit
still moves
around the places you loved
under the wings of owls

Here everything is kept precisely
the way I know
you would like it.
But for all my care

I know
that I will never be wakened again
to find you—
not even in this quivering in the air.

EVERY MONTH

The Ten-Year-Old Girl

My house
was close to the place where the bomb fell

My mother
was turned to white bone before
the family altar

Grandfather and I
go to visit her on the sixth of every month

Mother
is now living in the temple at Nakajima

Mother
must be so pleased
to see how big I've gotten

but all I see
is the Memorial Panel quietly standing there
no matter how I try
I can't remember what Mother looks like

EVERY YEAR

The Pastor

A great river runs through Hiroshima
and every year
we bring lanterns
inscribed with the names of the family dead

and light them and set them afloat—
lanterns
that carry the dead
vows of the living who will never forget

them and the way they died—
and for miles
the full breadth of the river is one
mass of flames.

THE VOICE UNDERNEATH
THE BURNING HOUSE

saying urgently:
Mother will come after you, Set-chan,
so you go away first.
Now quickly. Quickly.

Thirty-six years have passed
walking
        and lying down

alone
or in the arms of any man
I hear my mother shouting at me:

you go away
quickly!

THE GERMAN MISSIONARY

1.

Two men
were pushing a handcart up the sloping street—
chairs, hymnals, altar gear, the organ console—

carrying our church in pieces
out of Hiroshima—
and I was not with them.

I, John, sent into the mountains
before them, was building an altar
among pine roots

and I saw a blinding flash
cut across the sky
and there was a blank in time

2.

And the two men
that had fallen on their knees to cry
"Lord Jesus have pity on us!"

were immediately in the spirit
in the sheet of sun
in which they were taken

the moment of their vanishing
into prayer
printed on rock.

3.

This happened
thirty-six years ago:
the Power that binds

the atom ceased being invisible
and separated my brothers
from the shadows they cast

on a rock.
In the fan-shaped city
on the road to Koi

stands the rock.
And I go there each day
to bear witness.

V·Watchman:
from the Journals of
Nakajima Hiroshi

NIGHTWATCH

1.

During the war
I was made fire marshal
because I alone
of all the men in the neighborhood
had no office
or factory job to report to
by eight o'clock in the morning

If my luck had deserted me
I would have been lost

I went on doing what I always had done:

lying around the house
waking at noon
reading

going on aimless walks through the city

interfering with no one

as usual
I relieved my insomnia
by writing

only I didn't publish
my warnings

I lived for those diaries

I lived with them next to the pillow
just in case
I or they or both
needed saving

and I lived on my savings

when they ran out, my royalties
were good for some credit at the rice shop
when my books stopped selling
my friends left food at the door
when there was no food
we all starved
together

no one asked how many bottles
of ink I consumed
or where
they had come from or where
they had gone

it's amazing
how much you can hide
under a title

as fire marshal
everyone considered my behavior
proper
fully accounted for

the unusual hours
and the solitude of the task
were thought by many
to require an especially great personal sacrifice

I was praised accordingly

meanwhile
I went on taking three-hour-long hot baths

surely
some ironic god arranged my survival

in a police state
I, one of the few writers who failed
to exude patriotic gems
at a time
when silence was a punishable offense
and all my ex-comrades
had gone through the called-for
changes of heart—
I alone wasn't touched

months passed
I couldn't believe my good fortune

no raids
no interrogations
no beatings
were ordered to bring me into line

I
who at braver moments imagined myself ready to die
was never tested

2.

If I had tried to ingratiate myself
with the authorities
or the Japan Writers Patriotic Association
I would have lost
my smug look

my look of compliance
would have immediately fallen prey
to vigilance
and the stiff gestures
of one who is trying a little too hard

so the days
drifted into each other, and strangely
I couldn't get myself to do anything at all
to shore up my survival
I went on like this for years

even though I felt disfigured
by my passivity
even before I grasped
my planlessness, my living
from one moment to the next—

the one thing that could save me!

3.

Throughout the war
while others were being killed or jailed
for a word—a nuance—an impression
I was free
to stretch out whole afternoons
on a Western-style sofa, and chain-smoke
and write
the nightwatch away

toward dawn
I made my rounds through the sleeping city
and awakened no one

LAUDS

1.

Unable to sleep, during
the days of terror
that followed the bombing—

an old song repeated
itself in my head
till its words emptied

me of words, leaving
in their wake
a lullaby-belief in nothing
more than the daily round

2.

Rains will fall on the ruins
of the castle
as before

and trees will respond
each with its own kind of leaves
applauding the sun

3.

And when I stopped this chanting
and fell asleep
nothing could contain
my curses

SURRENDER

1.

The radio
they set up on an operating table
began to hum
and crackle

irregular spasms
of static
like the racket of crickets
in goose grass

or antiaircraft fire
faraway
then suddenly close—
a nerve-racking noise

only now and then
could I make out something
high-pitched and reedy—
a voice

talking court Japanese—
gobble
of archaic
"ye's" and whatnot

I caught only one phrase:
"Endure
the unendurable"—
then the static ceased

and the Chief of Communications
announced, "That broadcast
was in the Emporer's voice.
He said we have lost the war.

And we must be patient. We must
bow to necessity.
Until further notice
I want all of you to go about your duties."

2.

Lost! finally
everything's lost: family, home
country

General Anami has slit open his belly
according to custom

How foolish!

cigarettes will be plentiful
again

for the first time in four years
I can sit still, watching marvelous
calligraphy of smoke
drift off
into the daylight

FIRST TASTE OF PROSPERITY

Instead of the usual rations
each of us was given seven cartons of
Wrigley's Spearmint Gum

we chewed
until the sugar was out of it
then spit it out

unfolding and working through
new sticks
at the rate of fifty an hour

trying
to outpace the growling
of our stomachs.

I watched refugees
walk along, dropping
rubbery pellets and silver

gum wrappers, ceaselessly
chewing.
And though we worked our jaws

till they were numb
who could really silence
his hunger?

When would they give us rice?
No one asked.
But how hopefully we greeted

each convoy of jeeps!
The GIs beeped in their good-natured way
and waved their arms

there was a chorus of
"Hi!
How are you?"

and lines of frightened
beggars
immediately formed—

they were barraged with
Wrigley's,
with a shower of

thousands of packs
of spearmint chewing
gum.

Already
the American century was carpeting Japan
with peculiar abundance

the road to the A-bomb ward
was now paved
with silver.

RESPONSIBILITIES

When the moment came
I bent down
and removed the shoes from the feet
of a woman not yet

dead.
Glass scattered on the road—
in bare feet
I would never have escaped.

Responsibilities
can't be lopped off from the filthy
corpse-rich soil
in which they have their roots.

On the day I forget her
eyes
and begin to live
at peace with my memories

I will not recognize what
I am, pure
as a bone, and all my words
lies.

WALKING GHOSTS

Let the body
of writing that tells
their stories
fill with breath

robes
flap and bellow in the wind

look at these characters
raise their arms
and feet
as if to break out
of the white
sheets
where they can move once again

THE WITNESS

As I step off the platform
after reciting my poems

I am abashed

I feel more frail than ever

facing
the tears and gratitude I evoke
and my immense hunger
for both

suddenly
I can't tell
the difference between being
a profiteer
on the spiritual black market

and a prophet
who must tear everyone's heart
to shreds

as I wrote
I felt possessed by the dead calling
for peace

Now I wonder—

is it so laudable
to spend my days summoning
images of nuclear war?

yet how
can I give up
this fire
without betraying
myself and all that
I love

Notes

THIS BOOK IS BASED on testimony of survivors of Hiroshima and Nagasaki. Most of the poems, however, are neither versions of the actual or reinventions of the real; they are collages in which the actual and the imaginary freely mix, to give a vision of reality. Or, to paraphrase Marianne Moore, they present imaginary journeys with real pushcarts in them.

The relation of the poems to source materials varies considerably. It is not possible to notate the precise degree of indebtedness in each case, but certain distinctions can be made:

1. The term "follows closely" indicates that a poem is composed of an arrangement of fragments of a single source. The testimony of a single survivor, or a single account of survivors' experience, has been pared down, cut up, the elements mixed with a few minor additions, and given a new shape, a new rhythm.

2. The term "based on" indicates that a poem draws on two or more sources, that it is a collage in which the actual and the imaginary freely mix. In some poems, imaginary witnesses present imaginary narratives in which, here and there, actual details lie embedded; in others, actual witnesses are conflated to present actual events in which, here and there, imaginary details lie embedded. No formula, however, can be given for these poems.

3. The term "suggested by" indicates that some thought or image I came across in my reading played a part in the genesis of the poem.

QUESTIONS

Suggested, in part, by the phrase "selling the bomb" which recurs throughout Lifton's discussion of "Atomic Bomb Leaders," in *Death in Life*. See, for example, p. 214.

Nakajima Hiroshi's name is given in the Japanese order of surname followed by given name. The Western order is used for the other names in the book.

I. FIELD OF LOST EDGES

The three poems that form "Field of Lost Edges" are based, in part, on *The Day Man Lost*. See pp. 67–71, 73, 82, 92, 111–112, 114, 123, 144, 176, 179–181, 206–207, 227–228.

Section 1 of "New Year's Day, 1945" closely follows an entry in the wartime diary of Musei Tokugawa, quoted in *The Day Man Lost*, pp. 67–68.

Sections 1 and 6 of "May 7, 1945" are based, in part, on *Black Rain*, pp. 63–71 and 279–281, respectively.

II. THE PASSION

"The Bombing of Hiroshima"
Closely follows the testimony of the shopkeeper's assistant in *Death in Life*, p. 21.

"August 6, 1945"
Based on the testimony of the history professor in *Death in Life*, pp. 19 and 29, and on the description of the mushroom cloud in *Black Rain*, pp. 21–22.

"A White Blouse"
Based primarily on a sequence of drawings with accompanying narrative text by Tomoko Konishi in *Unforgettable Fire*, pp. 12–13, and on the narrative of the protagonist's escape from Yokogawa Station and his flight through the burning city in *Black Rain*, pp. 37–38, 49, 107, 121.
Section 1. Based on *Unforgettable Fire*, p. 12.
Section 2. Based on *Black Rain*, pp. 37–38.
Section 3. Closely follows *Black Rain*, p. 38.
Section 4. Based on *Black Rain*, p. 49.
Section 6. Closely follows *Unforgettable Fire*, p. 12.
Section 7. Closely follows *Nagasaki 1945*, pp. 58 and 79.
Section 8. Based on *Nagasaki 1945*, p. 58, on the testimony of the electrician in *Death in Life*, p. 24, and on Jacobo Timerman's "Reflections (Lebanon—Part I)," in *The New Yorker* (October 18, 1982), p. 82.
Section 9. Based on *Black Rain*, p. 121, and on "Summer Flower," p. 120.
Section 10. Follows *Unforgettable Fire*, p. 12.
Section 12. Based on *Unforgettable Fire*, p. 13.
Section 13. Based on *Black Rain*, p. 107.
Sections 14–16: Based on *Unforgettable Fire*, pp. 12–13.

"Encounter"
Based on an incident recounted in *Black Rain*, p. 51.
Section 1. Based on *Black Rain*, p. 51.
Section 2. Closely follows a comment made by the professor of English in *Death in Life*, p. 67.
Section 3. Suggested by *Black Rain*, p. 51.

"The Burden"

The central figure of this poem is a conflation of two of Hersey's hero-informants: the Reverend Kiyoshi Tanimoto, a pastor of the Hiroshima Methodist Church, and Father Wilhelm Kleinsorge, a German Jesuit.

Section 1. Based on *Hiroshima,* p. 38, and on *History and Human Survival,* p. 191.

Section 3. Based on *Hiroshima,* p. 38, and on *Black Rain,* pp. 44, 58, 79, 95, 99.

Section 4. Follows Hersey's account of the Reverend Mr. Tanimoto's flight into Hiroshima, in *Hiroshima,* pp. 39–40.

Section 5. Closely follows Hersey's account of Father Kleinsorge in Asano Park in *Hiroshima,* pp. 46–48. See also p. 59.

"Congregation"

The speaker of this poem is a conflation of four figures: the Reverend Mr. Tanimoto (*Hiroshima,* pp. 40 and 59), the Protestant minister (*Death in Life,* p. 38), Yoko Ōta (*Death in Life,* p. 56), and Hachirōyasutaka Ataga (*The Day Man Lost,* pp. 259–260).

Section 1. Based on *Hiroshima,* p. 40, and on *The Day Man Lost,* p. 259.

Section 2. Based on *The Day Man Lost,* pp. 259–260, and on *Death in Life,* p. 56.

Section 3. Based on *The Day Man Lost,* p. 260, on *Hiroshima,* p. 59, and on *Death in Life,* p. 38.

"Dragonflies"

The third stanza closely follows a passage in "Summer Flower," pp. 129–130.

III. DISTANCES

"Corpse Duty"

Follows the testimony of the social worker in *Death in Life,* pp. 31–32.

"The Walker"

The speaker of this poem is a conflation of the electrician and the history professor in *Death in Life,* p. 24 and p. 36, respectively.

"The Bones"

Section 2. Based on the testimony of the social worker in *Death in Life,* p. 67.

113

"The Homeowners"
Closely follows an incident recounted in *Black Rain,* p. 112.

"Them"
The speaker of this poem is a conflation of four figures: the electrician (*Death in Life,* p. 24), Dr. Michihiko Hachiya (*Hiroshima Diary,* pp. 54–55), the watch repairman (*Death in Life,* p. 25), and the grocer (*Death in Life,* p. 27).

This poem is also based on descriptions of survivors' behavior immediately after the bomb was dropped in *Black Rain,* pp. 44, 53, 55–57.

"The Doctor"
The first and third stanzas are near-verbatim quotations of the electrician and the doctor, respectively, in *History and Human Survival,* p. 165. The second stanza closely follows a passage in "Reflections: The Fate of the Earth (Part I)," *The New Yorker* (February 1, 1982), p. 76.

"Days of Terror"
Section 1. Based on *Nagasaki 1945,* pp. 117–118, and on *Hiroshima Diary,* p. 69.
Section 2. Based on *Hiroshima Diary,* pp. 12, 102.
Section 3. Based on *Nagasaki 1945,* p. 75, on *Hiroshima Diary,* pp. 61 and 185–186, and on the following passage on p. 4 of "Hiroshima Survivor," an unpublished paper by Setsuko Thurlo: "When at last [my sister and her four-year-old son] died, soldiers put their bodies in holes, doused them with gasoline, and cremated them. With my parents and just a few others, I stood watching the soldiers performing their tasks—poking the burning corpses with bamboo poles and making crude remarks."
Section 4. Based on *Hiroshima Diary,* p. 100.

"The Refugee"
Section 2. Closely follows a passage in *Black Rain,* pp. 143–144.

IV. In Mourning

"To Give Comfort"
Section 1. The comfort-giver's profession—scrivener—is that of Dr. Akizuki's father in *Nagasaki 1945,* p. 40.
Section 2. Based on *Hiroshima Diary,* pp. 68–69.
Section 3. Based, in part, on *Nagasaki 1945,* p. 52.

"Memory"

Section 3. The principal source of the remembered images is a drawing with accompanying text by Toraka Hironaka in *Unforgettable Fire*, pp. 26–27. The final image is a conflation of the picture of the burning hand and that of the dead baby in *Unforgettable Fire*, p. 96 and p. 104, respectively.

"Carrying My Brother"

Closely follows the testimony of the shopkeeper's assistant in *Death in Life*, p. 58.

"Every Day"

Suggested by the following lines in Kenneth Rexroth's translation of a poem by Hitomaro in *One Hundred Poems from the Japanese*, pp. 111–114:

In our bedroom our pillows
Lie side by side . . .
They tell me her spirit
May haunt Mount Hagai
Under the eagles' wings . . .
I know all the time
That I will never see her,
Not even so much as a faint quiver in the air. . . .

Section 1. Suggested, in part, by the following image in Israel Raphael's "Children of Immigration," in *The Book of Autobiographies*, p. 67: "On one side of the room was Papa's 'lunch.' This was how Papa pronounced his lounge, or couch. The leather covering still bore the indentations of his form from years of Sabbath siestas."

Section 2. Suggested, in part, by "The Journal of Margot Rodriguez," in *The Journal Project: Pages from the Lives of Old People*, p. 28.

"Every Month"

Closely follows the testimony of Sachiko Habu in *Children of the A-Bomb*, pp. 11–12.

"Every Year"

Closely follows a passage in E. P. Thompson's "A Letter to America," in *Protest and Survive*, p. 28.

"The Voice Underneath the Burning House"

The first stanza is a verbatim quotation of a child taken from *History and Human Survival*, p. 192.

"The German Missionary"

Suggested, in part, by the Book of Revelation and by the Reverend Mr. Tanimoto's piecemeal evacuation of the contents of his church in *Hiroshima*, pp. 3–4.

"There was a blank in time": this is a quotation of the history professor in *Death in Life*, p. 19.

V. WATCHMAN: FROM THE JOURNALS OF NAKAJIMA HIROSHI

"Nightwatch"

Suggested, in part, by the following passage in "The Camellia," p. 298: "I had been made fire marshal because I alone of the men in the neighborhood was at home in the daytime. Perhaps I was qualified too because, being of a timid nature, I did not make demands on people. I could read and write the night watch away, and it was my policy not to disturb people's sleep. I went my rounds and awakened no one, and fortunately in Kamakura that was enough."

Nakajima Hiroshi's wartime "silent protest" is based, in part, on that of Nagai Kafū as recounted in *Appreciations of Japanese Culture*, pp. 315–316.

"Lauds"

This poem was suggested by—and section 2 is based on—Dr. Akizuki's sudden remembrance of "an old poem, a fine piece of verse" which Dr. Hichiya—and no doubt countless other Japanese—also recalled after the Imperial Rescript ending the war. In *Nagasaki 1945*, p. 99, this poem is translated as follows: "A nation may be destroyed, yet its mountains and rivers will remain. Spring shall come to the ruins of the castle as before, and the grass and leaves will be thick and green again."

"Surrender"

Suggested, in part, by Lifton's discussion of "psychological non-resistance" in *Death in Life*, pp. 376–395.

Section 1. Based on *Hiroshima Diary*, p. 81, and *The Fall of Japan*, pp. 210–212. The final two stanzas in this section closely follow Chief Okamoto's statements in *Hiroshima Diary*, p. 81.

Section 2. Based, in part, on *Nagasaki 1945*, pp. 99–100.

"First Taste of Prosperity"

Based on "American *Hijiki*," pp. 444–445, 448, 455.

"The Witness"

Suggested, in part, by the following statement in Bruno Bettelheim's *Surviving and Other Essays*, p. 35: "I do not think it is particularly laudable to spend one's life bearing witness to the inhumanity of man to man." See also the note on "Questions."

Sources

Akizuki, Tatsuichiro. *Nagasaki 1945.* Translated by Keiichi Negata. Edited and with an Introduction by Gordon Honeycombe. London, Melbourne, New York: Quartet Books, 1981. (First published in 1945.)

Committee for the Compilation of Materials on Damage Caused by the Atomic Bombs in Hiroshima and Nagasaki. *Hiroshima and Nagasaki: The Physical, Medical and Social Effects of the Atomic Bombings.* Translated by Eisei Ishikawa and David L. Swain. New York: Basic Books, 1981.

Craig, William C. *The Fall of Japan.* New York: The Dial Press, 1967.

Hachiya, Michihiko. *Hiroshima Diary: The Journal of a Japanese Physician.* Translated and Edited by Warner Wells. Chapel Hill: The University of North Carolina Press, 1955.

Hara, Tamiki. "Summer Flower," in *The Catch and Other War Stories.* Selected and with an Introduction by Shōichi Saeki. Tokyo, New York, San Francisco: Kodansha, 1981.

Hearn, Lafcadio. *Kwaidan: Stories and Studies of Strange Things.* With an Introduction by Oscar Lewis. New York: Dover Publications, 1968. (First published in 1932.)

Hersey, John. *Hiroshima.* New York: Alfred A. Knopf, 1946.

Ibuse, Masuji. *Black Rain.* Translated by John Bester. New York, Tokyo, San Francisco: Kodansha, 1969.

Japan Broadcasting Corporation. *Unforgettable Fire: Pictures Drawn by Atomic Bomb Survivors.* New York: Pantheon Books, 1977.

Kawabata, Yasunari. "The Camellia," in *Contemporary Japanese Literature: An Anthology of Fiction, Film, and Other Writing Since 1945.* Translated by Edward Seidensticker. Edited by Howard Hibbett. New York: Alfred A. Knopf, 1982.

Keene, Donald. *Appreciations of Japanese Culture.* New York, Tokyo, San Francisco: Kodansha, 1981. (First published as *Landscapes and Portraits* in 1971.)

Kosaka, Masataka. *A History of Postwar Japan.* Foreword by Edwin O. Reischauer. Tokyo, New York, San Francisco: Kodansha, 1982. (First published as *One Hundred Millions Japanese* in 1972.)

Lifton, Robert Jay. *Death in Life: Survivors of Hiroshima*. New York: Simon and Schuster/A Touchstone Book, 1967.

———. *History and Human Survival*. New York: Vintage Books, 1971.

———. *The Broken Connection: On Death and the Continuity of Life*. New York: Simon and Schuster/A Touchstone Book, 1979.

———, Katō, Shūichi, and Reich, Michael R. *Six Lives/Six Deaths: Portraits from Modern Japan*. New Haven and London: Yale University Press, 1979.

Nosaka, Akiyuki. "American *Hijiki*," in *Contemporary Japanese Literature: An Anthology of Fiction, Film, and Other Writing Since 1945*. Translated by Jay Rubin. Edited by Howard Hibbett. New York: Alfred A. Knopf, 1982.

Osada, Arata. *Children of the A-Bomb: The Testament of the Boys and Girls of Hiroshima*. Translated by Jean Dan and Ruth Sieban-Morgan. New York: G. P. Putnam's Sons, 1963.

Pacific War Research Society. *Japan's Longest Day*. Tokyo, New York, San Francisco: Kodansha, 1980. (First published in 1965.)

———. *The Day Man Lost: Hiroshima, 6 August 1945*. Tokyo, New York, San Francisco: Kodansha, 1972.

Raphael, Israel. "Children of Immigration," in *The Book of Autobiographies*. Edited by Marc Kaminsky. New York: Teachers & Writers, 1982.

Rexroth, Kenneth. *One Hundred Poems from the Japanese*. New York: New Directions, 1964.

Rodriguez, Margot. "The Journal of Margot Rodriguez," in *The Journal Project: Pages from the Lives of Old People*. New York: Teachers & Writers, 1980.

Schell, Jonathan. *The Fate of the Earth*. New York: Alfred A. Knopf, 1982.

Stryk, Lucien. *Encounter with Zen: Writings on Zen and Poetry*. Chicago, London, and Athens, Ohio: Swallow Press and Ohio University Press, 1981.

Thompson, E. P., and Smith, Dan (eds.). *Protest and Survive*. New York and London: Monthly Review Press, 1981.

Thurlo, Setsuko. "Hiroshima Survivor," unpublished paper, 1982.